Research Methodology

RAJNISH MISHRA

To

My Bleloved Parents

Contents

Preface

This book is based upon my experience as a research student practitioner and teacher. Research Methodology is taught as a supporting subject in several ways in many Academic disciplines such as Management, Computer, Health, Education, Psychology, Social work, Library studies etc.

It is true that some discipline plays great emphasis on quantitative research and some qualitative research, but in my opinion research is the combination of both. This is meant for beginners.

I often obtain being approached by the students undergoing their project either in their bachelor's or in their master's courses in colleges, institutes and outside my own college, institute requesting to suggest a topic for their project, thesis, and dissertation. What should be carefully thought of critical the fact that students are not getting the training they need on research methodology so that they are empowered to handle most of these problems by themselves.

Traditionally, in India, a fairly good amount of research was being done in medical colleges. However, this scenario has now changed with Contract Reseach Organizations and Parmaceutical Companies doing most of the clinical trials and basic research, there has been a discernible fall in the quantity and quality of research.

It is no surprise that the Research Methodology has changed much in the past few decades.Publishing a scientific paper has also become more difficult as editors have beome more critical in accepting articles. In the light of these changes I believe that enough is not being done to help students approach plan and conduct their research in a scientific manner. The author is immensely thankful to all friends and discrete readers who will make constructive criticisms, suggestions for the improvement of the book.

The author gives special thanks to Publication Team.

Rajnish Mishra

Preface

1. Commercial and Business Research

Until the 1970s, the phrase 'qualitative research' was used only to refer to a discipline of anthropology or sociology. During the 1970s and 1980s qualitative research began to be used in other disciplines, and became a significant type of research in the fields of education studies, social work studies, women's studies, disability studies, information studies, management studies, nursing service studies, political science, psychology, communication studies, and many other fields. Qualitative research occurred in the consumer products industry during this period, with researchers investigating new consumer products and product positioning/advertising opportunities.

The earliest consumer research pioneers including Gene Reilly of The Gene Reilly Group in Darien, CT, Jerry Schoenfeld of Gerald Schoenfeld & Partners in Tarrytown, NY and Martin Calle of Calle & Company, Greenwich, CT, also Peter Cooper in London, England, and Hugh Mackay in Mission, Australia. There continued to be disagreement about the proper place of qualitative versus quantitative research. In the late 1980s and 1990s after a spate of criticisms from the quantitative side, new methods of qualitative research evolved, to address the perceived problems with reliability and imprecise modes of data analysis. During this same decade, there was a slowdown in traditional media advertising spending, so there was heightened interest in making research related to advertising more effective.

In the present fast track business environment marked by cutthroat competition, many organizations rely on business research to gain a competitive advantage and greater market share. Business Research is the pursuit of truth with the help of study, observation, comparison and experiment. The search for knowledge through objective and systematic method of finding solution to a problem. To discover answers to questions through the application of scientific procedures. To find out the truth which is hidden and which has not been discovered as yet. To gain familiarity with a phenomenon. To portray accurately the characteristics of a particular individual, situation or a group.

The business world is becoming increasingly competitive due to rapid advancement of Internet technologies whereby many business organizations have incorporated the web as the new marketing channel to reach out for their stake holders in the global market, particularly the suppliers and the customers.

Many companies are finding it difficult to sustain competitive advantage in today's markets as more and more new entries are competing in the same market segment, also known as the red ocean market which has become overcrowded and profits are thinning.

With the looming of the possible recession facing the largest economy in the world and possibly the whole world, the future of business organizations look groom and many of them will finally collapse if nothing is done about it. So, the big question how does the business organizations survive in such troubling time?

A lot of what we do in our daily lives is based on common sense, what we have learnt from others or what we have learnt through personal experience or observation. But sometimes common sense is not the best approach and sometimes there are conflicting theories about what is best or what works in a particular situation.

Moreover, what works in one situation or for one condition might be ineffective or even dangerous in another, or when combined with other measures. Common sense approaches may overlook the impact of external factors which may contribute to what is observed.

Even in the domain of healthcare, there are gaps in knowledge, theories about how something might work better and ideas for improvement. In research some methods and principles are to be followed the following 360 degree of Research Methodology helps you in understanding the whole process of research.

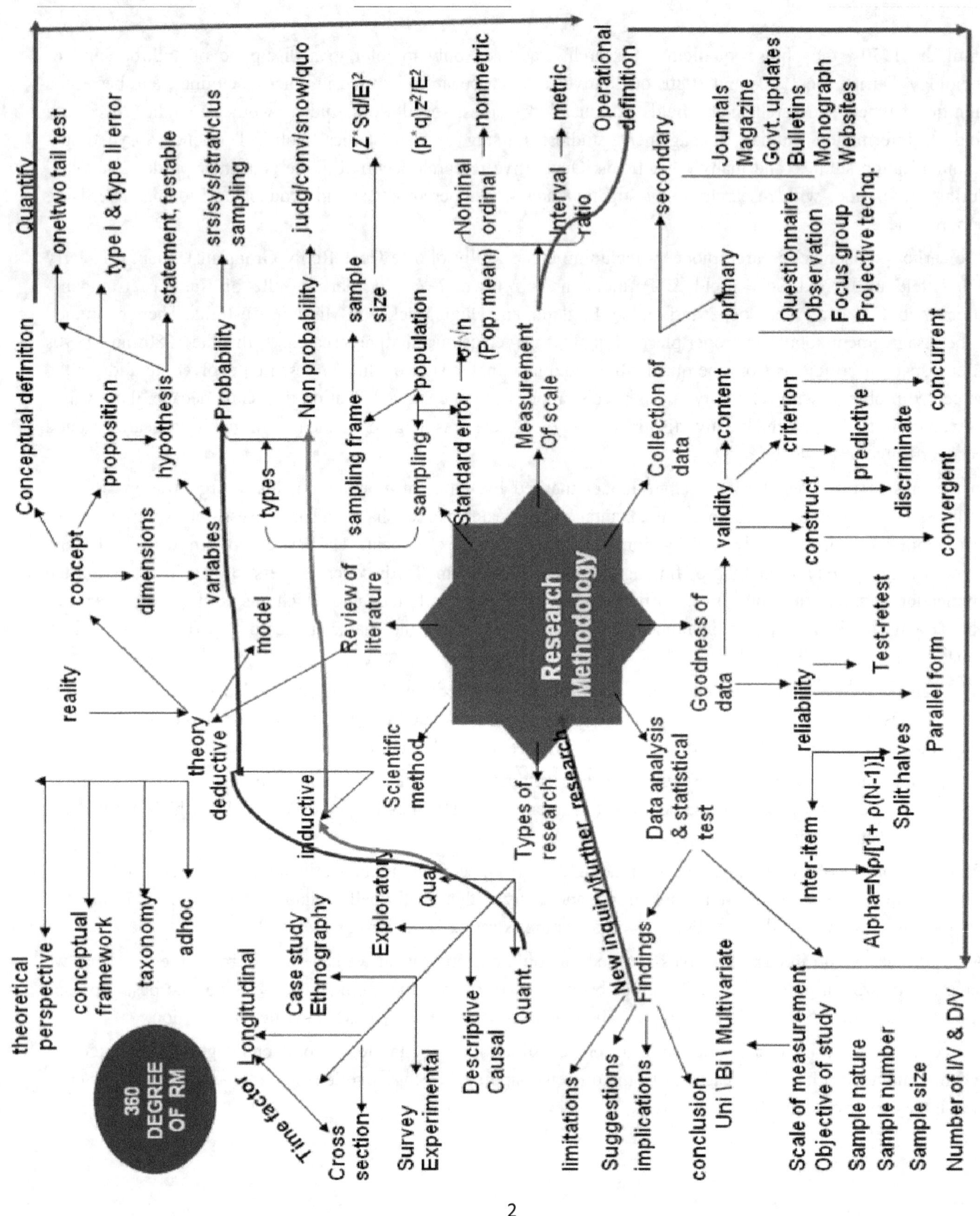

1.1 Meaning of Research

Any study to create new knowledge or aims to increase existing fund of knowledge may it be through observation or by some other methods, is called research if it takes into account the biases, the errors and limitations. As such, research may be described as systematic and critical investigation of phenomena toward increasing the stream of knowledge.

1. Research simply means a search for facts- answers to question and solutions to   problems.
2. It is a purposive investigation.
3. It is organized inquiry.

Research is:

- An active, diligent, and systematic process of inquiry aimed at discovering, interpreting and revising facts.
- An organised, systematic, data-based critical scientific inquiry or investigation into a specific problem, undertaken with the objective of finding answers or solutions to it.
- This intellectual investigation produces a greater understanding of events, behaviours, or theories, and makes practical applications through laws and theories.
- Also used to describe a collection of information about a particular subject, and is usually associated with science and the scientific method.

1.2 Aims

The aims of research are to unravel the mysteries of nature, aquire knowledge for its own sake and extend the frontiers of knowledge. Research is really np0t concerned with the utilization of the knowledge so gained.

1.3 Objectives or Process of research *(According to C. R. Kothari)*

1. Research extends knowledge of human beings, social life and environment. Scientists and researchers build up the wealth of knowledge through their research findings. They search answers for various types of questions: What, Where, When, How and Why of various phenomena and enlighten us.
2. Research unravels the mysteries of nature; brings to light hidden information that might never be discovered fully during the ordinary course of life.
3. Research establishes generalizations and general laws and contributes to theory building in various fields of knowledge.
4. Research verifies and tests existing facts and theory and help improving our knowledge and ability to handle situations and events.
5. Research also aims at developing new tools, concepts, and theories for better study of unknown phenomena.

Motivation in Research *(According to C. R. Kothari)*

1. Desire to get a research degree along with its consequential benefits.
2. Desired to face the challenge in solving the unsolved problems, i.c., concern over practical problems initiates research.
3. Desire to get intellectual joy of doing some creative work.
4. Desire to be of service to society.
5. Desire to get responsibility.

Types of Research

According to the intent:

1. Pure Research
2. Applied Research
3. Exploratory Research
4. Descriptive Study
5. Diagnostic Study
6. Evaluation Studies
7. Action Research

1. Pure Research

Pure research is undertaken for the sake of knowledge without any intention to apply it in practice, e.g., Einstein's theory of relativity, Newton's contributions.

2. Applied Research

Applied research is carried on to find solution to a real-life problem requiring an action or policy decision. It is problem-oriented and action-directed.

3. Exploratory Research

It is preliminary study of an unfamiliar problem about which the researcher has little or no knowledge. It is similar to doctor's initial investigation.

4. Descriptive Study

It is a fact-finding investigation with adequate interpretation. It is the simplest type of research.

5. Diagnostic Study

This is similar to descriptive study but with a different focus. It is directed towards discovering what is happening, why is it happening and what can be done about. It aims at identifying the causes of problem and the possible solutions for it.

6. Evaluation Studies

It is one type of applied research. It is made for assessing the effectiveness of social or economic programmes implemented (e.g., family planning scheme) or for assessing the impact of developmental projects (e.g., irrigation project) on the development of the project area.

7. Action Research

It is a type of evaluation study. It is a concurrent evaluation study of an action programme launched for solving a problem/for improving an existing situation.

According to the methods of study:
1. Experimental Research
2. Analytical Study
3. Historical Research
4. Survey

1. Experimental Research

It is designed to assess the effects of particular variables on a phenomenon by keeping the other variables constant or controlled. It aims at determining whether and in what manner variables are related to each other.

2. Analytical Study

It is a system of procedures and techniques of analysis applied to quantitative data. It may consist of system of mathematical models or statistical techniques applicable to numerical data. Hence, it is also known as the Statistical Method.

3. Historical Research

It is a study of past records and other information sources with a view to reconstructing the origin and development of an institution or movement or a system and discovering the trends in the past.

4. Survey

It is a factfinding study. It is a method of research involving collection of data directly from a population or a sample thereof at particular time.

Goals of Research

The goals of research can be classified into two categories, namely, (a) Theory Building/ Generation of Knowledge, and (b) Problem Identification and Problem Solving. The dissertations for Masters, M.Phil. and Doctoral degrees are intended to generate knowledge where as intervention research, action research and diagnostic research basically aim at problem solving.

Marketing / Business Research

Marketing / business research concerns with issues pertaining to marketing/business, such as, market potential, market share, image, sales analysis, forecasting, trends, products, pricing, promotion, distribution, business trends, finance, productivity, human resource, organisational behaviour, etc.

1.4 Importance – Research methodology

The role of research has greatly increased in the field of business and economy as a whole. The study of research methods provides you with the knowledge and skills you need to solve the problems and meet the challenges of today's modern pace of development. Three factors stimulate the interest in a scientific research to decision making:

1. The manager's increased need for more and better information.
2. The availability of improved techniques and tools to meet this need.
3. The resulting information overloads.

The following are the areas in which research methodology can help in better decision making:

1. Marketing Research
2. Government Policies and Economic System
3. Solving Various Operational and planning Problems of Business and Industry
4. Social Relationship

1.5 Research Plan or design-steps

Step 1: Identification of a Research Problem.

Selecting a Research Problem

The first hurdle confronting a researcher is to select a topic that is appropriate for scientific inquiry. Actually, this is not as difficult as it may fist appear because the world around us is literally full of unanswered questions. Selecting a problem calls for some creativity and imagination, but there are also a number of sources you can look for inspiration. Some of the more common sources of research problems are discussed here.

Step 2: Define the Research Topic

Once a research problem has been identified, the research topic needs to be defined. Research topic should be defined in such a way that it is clearly understood.

If you are studying, say for example, alcoholism; you need to put your research question into a framework which suggests that you are very clear and specific about the problem of alcohol consumption and abuse. In short, topics of research must be grounded in some already-known factual information which is used to introduce the topic and from which the research question will emerge.

Step 3: Review of Existing Literature

Research topics are usually embedded in so many different kinds of literature that the researcher must be careful in to selecting the best literature to examine. While many researchers collect every material, which has some linkages with the topic, you need to keep the central theme of your topic in mind to guide you through your search of the literature in the field. It is also important to examine different types of literature where relevant inferences are drawn from scientific data interpretations. It would be very useful if research findings from studies using various methods are critically examined.

Step 4: Identifications of Objectives of the Study

Once the problem, the theoretical background, the clarification of concepts, and the major methods of data collection have been explained, it is time to address the aim and objectives of the study.

At this stage you are required to present the aim and the objectives of the study in brief justify your study in terms of both its rationale and the implications that it might raise. But in a proposal the study design must be presented before the rationale Here it is important to note that   rationale for doing the project will be accomplished only if the study is done well. Preparing a plan of your study will show that you have devised a plan to study your problem that seems feasible; you reinforce the sense that the aims and objectives of the study will be achieved. The value of the study lies not only in what it alone will produce, but also in how it may add to or challenge other research in the area.

Step 5: Formulation of Hypotheses

A common strategy in scientific study is to move from a general theory to a specific researchable problem. A part of this exercise is to develop hypotheses, which are testable statements of presumed relationships between two or more variables. Hypotheses state what we expect to find rather than what has already been determined to exist. For example, we might hypothesise that the acceptance of the use of alcohol among adolescent's peers will lead to increased likelihood that the adolescents will consume alcohol.

Step 6: Selection of Method of Data Collection

There are three primary means of data collection, namely, observation, interview and questionnaire. While preparing the research plan you must describe how you will collect primary data. In case you are planning to use secondary data, you must mention which sources of available data you will actually use. You may also very briefly discuss about issues of access to the data. It is important for a researcher to see that, he/she must be able to get the data he/she proposes. If you anticipate problems in securing the proposed data, these problems should be discussed and possible alternate sources of data might be suggested. Most researchers propose to use one source of data yet you maypropose few more sources through which you may also collect data from other sources to widen their scope.

Step 7: Selection of Sample

The selection of sample whom you will study depends on many factors and it is not possible to take into account all. However, there are some factors which affect the selection of the sample to a great extent. We will discuss a few of them. The homogeneity or heterogeneity of the universe is one such factor which affects the sample selection procedure to a great extent. For example, if you are interested in studying medical students, which is a very homogeneous group, even a very small ample will be representative of the universe where as if you plan to study a college having arts, science and commerce faculties you may have to chose a very large sample and even then you may not have confidence to say that your sample is representative.

You may be interested in generalizing your findings to others beyond those studied. When probability samples are used, it is possible to determine how representative your sample is of the population who might have gotten into your study. Sampling plans may be very simple or complex. When the rules of probability are not followed and you merely select a sample of subjects who seem to fulfill the needs of your study, you have a non-probability sample. For many studies, such a sample is sufficient; and for some, it is the best that can be achieved. Whatever the design of your sample, it needs to be explained in detail in your research plan. It should be so precise that someone else

could generate a similar sample by following your procedures. Remember that even if you select a representative sample you have to be very careful in making generalisations.

Step 8: Collection of Data

There are different methods of data collection. Each method of data collection has its special concerns which need to be considered fully before doing the study. This is why pre-testing is so valuable, because it helps you to find and address potential problems before they enter your study and cause bigger problems.

The plans for collecting data should be described carefully. In a field study, it is always more difficult to be precise, and you may need to make changes once you enter the field. Nevertheless, it is better to have a clear plan that can be changed as you move forward for an experiment; data collection procedures can usually be described very precisely. This is also true of a survey. Surveys using mailed questionnaire tend to have multiple stages in the data collection procedure to increase the *response rate*. If you are using secondary data, you need to describe at this stage how you will collect the data.

Step 9: Processing of the Data

Once the data are collected, they must be processed. If the responses are in qualitative terms you have to prepare a codebook where you have to give numbers for the qualitative responses. This very much essential if you wish to process your data through computer. If they are field notes, they must be organized and categorized.

In the research plan, a concise statement may be included to address this subject. It may describe what type of computer facilities is available, what possible sources of assistance are available, and what efforts are being made to increase accuracy in the handling of the data. There are now some technological advances in data gathering which speed the process from data gathering to data entry. An example is the SPSS (Statistical Package for Social Sciences) now becoming quite common for research.

Step 10: Analysis of the Data

We need to plan how we will analyze the data. It is advisable to prepare a plan of analysis of data spelling out the various applications of statistical tests carefully while the study is being designed. It is better to have a planned strategy that can be adapted than to end up with piles of data for which you have no organized plan.

In addition, you need to consider which statistical tests you plan to apply to evaluate the association / differences between the variables .For example, if you propose to measure correlation between the variables to test whether there are significant correlations between them you have to select an appropriate test of correlation that could get the result you need.

Step 11: Writing of Report

At the end of the study, you have to present the results of the study in the form of a report. While preparing a research report you have to follow a number of writing conventions. These conventions are commonly known as research formats.

Reasearch Designs

A research design is the logical and systematic plan of carrying out research. The design results from translating a general scientific model into varied research problems. Research design is a detailed plan outlining how the research will be carried out. Thus, the details about these issues constitute a research design. To be more specific, a research design includes the details about the purpose of research, area of study (population), sampling plan, method and techniques of data collection and analytic design.

 In fact, the research design spells out in considerable detail what occur in the following steps of the research process.

Exploratory Research

The purpose of exploratory studies is to formulate a problem for a more precise investigation or to develop hypotheses. However, an exploratory study can also be conducted to enhance the familiarity of researcher with the phenomena, he/she wishes to study some time later in a more scientific way.

For instance, a researcher might wish to find out which all factors /attributes are used in purchase decision; how the consumers are influenced by the different forms of communications or what is the possible explanation for a given marketing phenomenon (say, sales drop) and establish priorities for future research. A manufacturer faced with decreased sales might conduct an exploratory research to generate possible explanations.

Conclusive Research

Conclusive research is typically more formal and structured than exploratory research. It is based on large, representative samples, and the data obtained are subjected to quantitative analysis. The findings from this research are considered to be conclusive in nature in that they are used as input into managerial decision making.

Descriptive Research Designs

Descriptive studies, as name suggests, describe as accurately as possible the characteristics of a group of people or a community. A researcher who is interested in studying people of a community, their age and sex composition, caste wise distribution, affiliation to religion, level of education, occupational status, designs his study as descriptive study. Another researcher may formulate a descriptive design of study to know the proportion of people in a particular population who favours dowry or who feels that child labour should be banned. Still others may be concerned with specific prediction. For example, what percentage of population would enter voter's list in the next census operations? What will be the size of the handicapped population who will need financial assistance in the next five-year plan? And so on.

Cross –sectional Research Design

A researcher collects data for his/her research at one point of time. This research design is most frequently used by researchers because it is the simplest and least costly alternative. The most striking disadvantage of this research design is that it cannot cover processes or change.

Longitudinal Research Design

To describe the changes in the features of a market phenomenon longitudinal research designs are used. In this research designs the phenomenon is studied at more than one time. It is usually more complex and costly than cross-sectional research designs. It is also more powerful, especially when researchers seek answers to questions about market change.

Causal Research Design

When we have a problem that is already known and have a description of it, we may like to know why things are the way they are. The purpose of causal research is to explain "why". In causal research, the researcher goes beyond focusing on a topic or portraying it. He or she looks for causes and their effects and their relationships.

Experimental Research Designs

By and large, experimental studies are concerned with testing of causal hypothesis. A casual hypotheses refers to causal relationships between two variables where one variable. For example, if a researcher wishes to test a causal hypothesis that punishments (X) cause low self-esteem (Y) by comparing a group of students who have been exposed to punishments (X) with one that has not been exposed, he has to measure the two groups with respect of Y, either during or after exposure to X.

Before discussing about the various types of experimental studies used for testing the causal relationship it is essential to know about the concept of causality.

The Logic of Causal Inference

To clarify the issues raised above, we have to understand the logic of causal inference. The three conditions that have to be fulfilled to draw a causal inference are:

If   (1)   the cause precedes the effect in time,

      (2)   there is an empirical correlation between them, and

      (3)   the relationship is not found to be the result of the effects of some third variable on each of the two initially observed.

The first condition in a causal relationship is that the cause precedes the effect in time. For example, in the game of snooker the first impulsion is the cause of movements of the second ball and the subsequent balls. The movements of second and subsequent balls are the effect of the cause induced by the impulsion.

The second condition in a causal relationship is that the two variables be empirically correlated with one another. For example, if a researcher wishes to examine if there is cause-effect relationship between gender and achievement, he or she has to use correlational technique to assess the magnitude of the relationship. It is also required that the coefficient of correlation is substantial.

The third condition for a causal relationship is that the observed empirical correlation between two variables cannot be explained away as being due to the influence of some third variable that causes both of them. For example, it may be observed that there is a strong correlation between 'knee joints pain' and 'amount of rainfall' but this does not mean that joints pain effect rainfall. A third variable, relative humidity is the cause of both knee joints pain and rainfall. Any relationship satisfying all these conditions is causal, and these are the only conditions of cause –effect relationship.

Types of Experimental Research Designs

There are a large number of experimental designs. Various authors have grouped experimental designs into certain categories based on extent of control. Most common grouping comprises:

- True Experimental Designs,
- Pre-Experimental Designs, and
- Quasi Experimental designs

True Experimental Designs

True Experimental Designs have maximum control and hence highest degree of internal validity. The essential components of an experimental research design involve (a) random assignments of subjects to experimental and control groups, (b) introducing the stimulus (independent variable) to the experimental group while withholding it from the control group, and (c) comparing the amount of change in dependent variable in experimental and control groups.

Pre-Test - Posttest- Control Group Design

The classic experimental design, which is also known as pre-test-post–test control group design can be shown in shorthand notation as:

$$E \longrightarrow R \longrightarrow Y_1 \longrightarrow X \longrightarrow Y_2$$

$$C \longrightarrow R \longrightarrow Y'_1 \longrightarrow \text{Non- } X \longrightarrow Y'_2$$

E and C represent experimental group and control groups respectively. R stands for random assignments of subjects to either experimental group or the control group.

The notation X represents the introduction of a stimulus, $Y1'_s$ represents pretests and the Y_2·s represents posttests. In this design, experimental group and the control group subjects are measured on a dependent variable before and after the introduction of stimulus.

Pre-Experimental Designs

Research designs in which most of the sources of internal and external validity are not controlled are termed as Pre-Experimental Research Designs. These designs are the weakest kind of research designs. In fact, the risk of drawing causal inference from these designs is extremely high. Still they are used quite often in research. These designs help to illustrate the advantages of experimental research designs.

One Shot Case Study

The shorthand notation for One Shot Case Study design is:

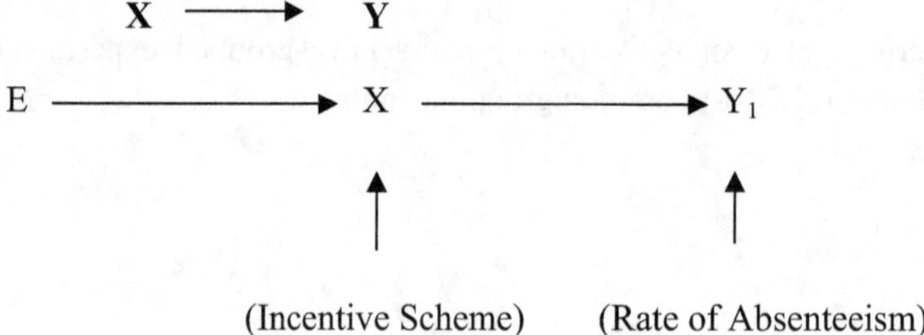

Quasi-Experimental Research Designs

Many a times, it is not possible to achieve random assignments of subjects to experimental and control groups and withhold stimulus (intervention) to one group (control group). In such cases, instead of foregoing the study altogether, it is sometimes possible to create and execute alternative research designs that have less internal validity than experimental research designs but still provide reasonably good amount of evidences for causal inferences. These designs are called quasi-experimental research designs and are distinguished from experimental research designs due to lack of random assignments of subjects to experimental and control groups. In this section, we will discuss some quasi-experimental research designs that are applicable to research.

This research design is commonly called as Pre-test Post-test Non-equivalent Control Group Design and can be symbolized as follows:

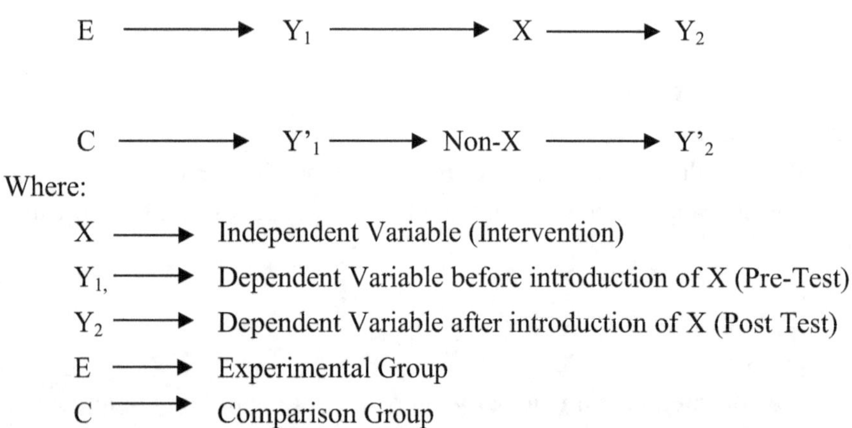

Where:

X ⟶ Independent Variable (Intervention)

Y_1, ⟶ Dependent Variable before introduction of X (Pre-Test)

Y_2 ⟶ Dependent Variable after introduction of X (Post Test)

E ⟶ Experimental Group

C ⟶ Comparison Group

Time-Series Designs

When comparison group is not available for assessing cause-effect relationship - Time-Series Designs can be used. In Time-Series Designs pretest and posttest measures are taken a number of times before and after the introduction of stimulus. Usually the researcher attempts to obtain at least five sets of measures before and after the introduction of independent variable. A typical time series design can be represented as follows:

$$Y_1 \quad Y_2 \quad Y_3 \quad Y_4 \quad Y_5 \quad X \quad Y_6 \quad Y_7 \quad Y_8 \quad Y_9 \quad Y_{10}$$

Where:

Y_1 to Y_5 $\longrightarrow$ Measurements of $_{Dependent}$ Variable before introduction of X   (Pre-Test)

X $\longrightarrow$ Independent Variable (Intervention: Counselling)

Y_6 to Y_{10} $\longrightarrow$ Measurements of $_{Dependent}$ Variable after introduction of X (Post -Test)

2. Research Process

Conducting research involves using the scientific method at its core. Therefore, before any research is undertaken, it is important to be aware of the steps. The research methodology has not come up overnight, but has evolved through hundreds of years of science. The history of science is interesting and intriguing, giving an insight into the developments of modern-day science. There are several pioneers who shaped the current research process. You may like to look at who invented the scientific method to get an idea of the early scientists and the influence they have, directly or indirectly, on what every researcher does today.

At the heart of the research methodology, is the fundamental and lingering question of the definition of research. This is by no means a trivial question and the answer constantly keeps evolving with time. To understand the world around us, the researcher needs to know and understand the definition of the scientific method. This will be central to the research process and subsequent conclusions drawn from the experiment.

Research Process

Everybody collects, interprets and uses information, much of it in a numerical or statistical form in day-to-day life. It is a common practice that people receive large quantities of information every day through conversations, televisions, computers, the radios, newspapers, posters, notices and instructions. It is just because there is so much information available that people need to be able to absorb, select and reject it.

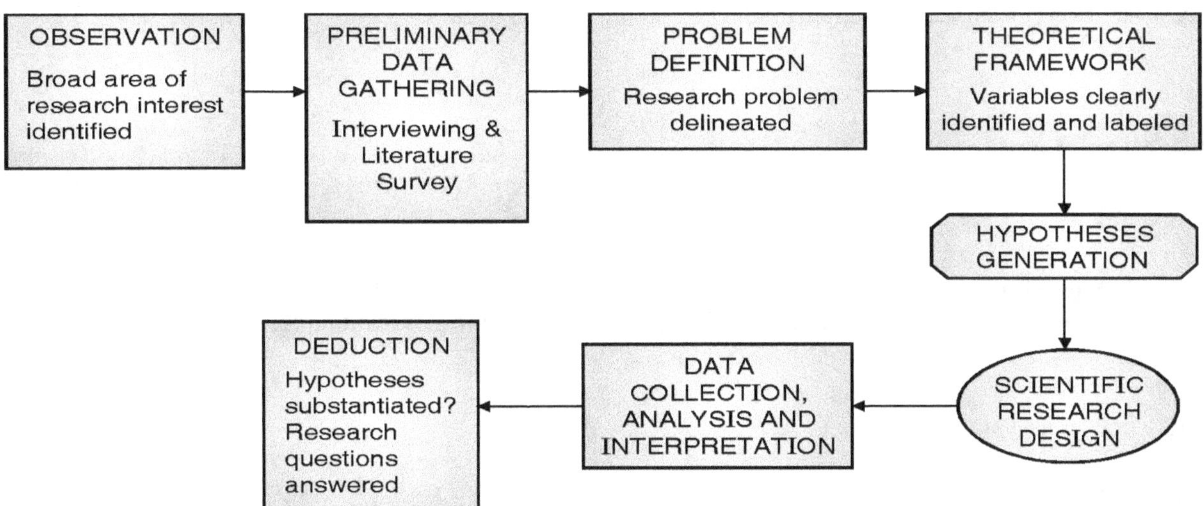

In everyday life, in business and industry, certain statistical information is necessary and it is independent to know where to find it how to collect it. As consequences, everybody has to compare prices and quality before making any decision about what goods to buy. As employees of any firm, people want to compare their salaries and working conditions, promotion opportunities and so on. In time the firms on their part want to control costs and expand their profits. One of the main functions of statistics is to provide information which will help on making decisions. Statistics provides the type of information by providing a description of the present, a profile of the past and an estimate of the future.

The following are some of the objectives of collecting statistical information -

1.   To describe the methods of collecting primary statistical information.

2.   To consider the status involved in carrying out a survey.

3.   To analyse the process involved in observation and interpreting.

4.   To define and describe sampling.

5.   To analyse the basis of sampling.

6.   To describe a variety of sampling methods.

Statistical investigation is a comprehensive and requires systematic collection of data about some group of people or objects, describing and organizing the data, analyzing the data with the help of different statistical method, summarizing the analysis and using these results for making judgements, decisions and predictions. The validity and accuracy of final judgement is most crucial and depends heavily on how well the data was collected in the first place. The quality of data will greatly affect the conditions and hence at most importance must be given to this process and every possible precaution should be taken to ensure accuracy while collecting the data.

2.1 Collecting Data

Nature of data:

It may be noted that different types of data can be collected for different purposes. The data can be collected in connection with time or geographical location or in connection with time and location. The following are the three types of data:

1. Time series data.

2. Spatial data

3. Spacio-temporal data.

1. **Time series data:**

It is a collection of a set of numerical values, collected over a period of time. The data might have been collected either at regular intervals of time or irregular intervals of time.

Example 1:

The following is the data for the three types of expenditures in rupees for a family for the four years 2001,2002,2003,2004.

YEAR	FOOD	EDUCATION	OTHERS	TOTAL
2001	2000	1500	4000	7500
2002	3000	2000	5000	10000
2003	4000	2500	6000	12500
2004	5000	3500	4000	12500

2. Spatial Data:

If the data collected is connected with that of a place, then it is termed as spatial data. For example, the data may be

1. Number of runs scored by a batsman in different test matches in a test series at different places
2. District wise rainfall in Maharashtra
3. Prices of silver in four metropolitan cities

Example 2:

The population of the southern states of India in 1991.

State	Population
Andhra Pradesh	6,63,04,854
Karnataka	4,48,17,398
Kerala	2,90,11,237
Tamilnadu	5,56,38,318
Pondicherry	7,89,416

3. Spacio Temporal Data:

If the data collected is connected to the time as well as place then it is known as spacio temporal data.

Example 3:

State	Population	
	1981	**1991**
Tamil Nadu	4,82,97,456	5,56,38,318
Andhra Pradesh	5,34,03,619	6,63,04,854
Karnataka	3,70,43,451	4,48,17,398
Kerala	2,54,03,217	2,90,11,237
State	6,04,136	7,89,416

2.2 Categories of data:

Any statistical data can be classified under two categories depending upon the sources utilized. These categories are-

1. Primary data
2. Secondary data

2.2.1 Primary data:

Primary data is the one, which is collected by the investigator himself for the purpose of a specific inquiry or study. Such data is original in character and is generated by survey conducted by individuals or research institution or any organization.

Example 4:

If a researcher is interested to know the impact of noon-meal scheme for the school children, he has to undertake a survey and collect data on the opinion of parents and children by asking relevant questions. Such a data collected for the purpose is called primary data.

The primary data can be collected by the following five methods.

1. Direct personal interviews.
2. Indirect Oral interviews.
3. Information from correspondents.
4. Mailed questionnaire method.
5. Schedules sent through enumerators.

1. Direct personal interviews:

The person from whom informations are collected are known as informants. The investigator personally meets them and asks questions to gather the necessary informations. It is the suitable method for intensive rather than extensive field surveys. It suits best for intensive study of the limited field.

Merits:

1. People willingly supply informations because they are approached personally. Hence, more response noticed in this method than in any other method.

2. The collected informations are likely to be uniform and accurate. The investigator is there to clear the doubts of the informants.

3. Supplementary informations on informant's personal aspects can be noted. Informations on character and environment may help later to interpret some of the results.

4. Answers for questions about which the informant is likely to be sensitive can be gathered by this method.

5. The wordings in one or more questions can be altered to suit any informant.

Limitations:

1. It is very costly and time consuming.
2. It is very difficult, when the number of persons to be interviewed is large and the persons are spread over a wide area.
3. Personal prejudice and bias are greater under this method.

2. Indirect Oral Interviews:

Under this method the investigator contacts witnesses or neighbours or friends or some other third parties who are capable of supplying the necessary information.This method is preferred if the required information is on addiction or cause of fire or theft or murder etc., If a fire has broken out a certain place, the persons living inneighbourhood and witnesses are likely to give information on the cause of fire.

In some cases, police interrogated third parties who are supposed to have knowledge of a theft or a murder and get some clues. Enquiry committees appointed by governments generally adopt this method and get people's views and all possible details of facts relating to the enquiry. This method is suitable whenever direct sources do not exists or cannot be relied upon or would be unwilling to part with the information.

The validity of the results depends upon a few factors, such as the nature of the person whose evidence is being recorded, the ability of the interviewer to draw out information from the third parties by means of appropriate questions and cross examinations, and the number of persons interviewed. For the success of this method one person or one group alone should not be relied upon.

3. Information from correspondents:

The investigator appoints local agents or correspondents in different places and compiles the information sent by them. Informations to Newspapers and some departments of Government come by this method. The advantage of this method is that it is cheap and appropriate for extensive investigations. But it may not ensure accurate results because the correspondents are likely to be negligent, prejudiced and biased. This method is adopted in those cases where informations are to be collected periodically from a wide area for a long time.

4. Mailed questionnaire method:

Under this method a list of questions is prepared and is sent to all the informants by post.The list of questions is technically called questionnaire.   A covering letter accompanying the questionnaire explains the purpose of the investigation and the importance of correct informations and request the informants to fill in the blank spaces provided and to return the form within a specified time.   This method is appropriate in those cases where the informants are literates and are spread over a wide area.

Merits:

1.   It is relatively cheap.
2.   It is preferable when the informants are spread over the wide area.

Limitations:

1.   The greatest limitation is that the informants should be literates who are able to understand and reply the questions.
2.   It is possible that some of the persons who receive the questionnaires do not return them.
3.   It is difficult to verify the correctness of the information furnished by the respondents.

With the view of minimizing   non-respondents and collecting correct   information, the questionnaire should be carefully drafted. There is no hard and fast rule. But the following general principles may be helpful in framing the questionnaire. A covering letter and a self addressed and stamped envelope should accompany the questionnaire. The covering letter should politely point out the purpose of the survey and privilege of the respondent who is one among the few associated with the investigation. It should assure that the information would be kept confidential and would never be misused. It may promise a copy of the findings or free gifts or concessions etc.

Characteristics of a good questionnaire:

1.   Number of questions should be minimum.
2.   Questions should be in logical orders, moving from easy to more difficult questions.
3.   Questions should be short and simple.
4.   Questions fetching YES or NO answers are preferable. There may be some multiple choice questions requiring lengthy answers are to be avoided.
5.   Personal questions and questions which require memory power and calculations should also be avoided.
6.   Question   should enable cross check. Deliberate or unconscious mistakes can be detected to an extent.
7.   Questions should be carefully framed so as to cover the entire scope of the survey.
8.   The wording of the questions should be proper without hurting the feelings or arousing resentment.
9.   As far as possible confidential informations should not be sought.
10.   Physical appearance should be attractive, sufficient space should be provided for answering each questions.

Limitations:

1. It is the costliest method.
2. Extensive training is to be given to the enumerators for collecting correct and uniform informations.
3. Interviewing requires experience. Unskilled investigators are likely to fail in their work.

Before the actual survey, a pilot survey is conducted. The questionnaire/schedule is pre-tested in a pilot survey. A few among the people from whom actual information is needed are asked to reply. If they misunderstand a question or find it difficult to answer or do not like its wordings etc., it is to be altered. Further it is to be ensured that every questions fetches the desired answer.

Merits and Demerits of primary data:

1. The collection of data by the method of personal survey is possible only if the area covered by the investigator is small. Collection of data by sending the enumerator is bound to be expensive. Care should be taken twice that the enumerator record correct information provided by the informants.
2. Collection of primary data by framing a schedules or distributing and collecting questionnaires by post is less expensive and can be completed in shorter time.
3. Suppose the questions are embarrassing or of complicated nature or the questions probe into personnel affairs of individuals, then the schedules may not be filled with accurate and correct information and hence this method is unsuitable.
4. The information collected for primary data is mere reliable than those collected from the secondary data.

2.2.2 Secondary Data:

Secondary data are those data which have been already collected and analysed by some earlier agency for its own use; and later the same data are used by a different agency. According to W.A.Neiswanger, ' A primary source is a publication in which the data are published by the same authority which gathered and analysed them. A secondary source is a publication, reporting the data which have been gathered by other authorities and for which others are responsible.

Sources of Secondary data :

In most of the studies the investigator finds it impracticable to collect first-hand information on all related issues and as such he makes use of the data collected by others. There is a vast amount of published information from which statistical studies may be made and fresh statistics are constantly in a state of production. The sources of secondary data can broadly be classified under two heads:

1. Published sources, and
2. Unpublished sources.

1. Published Sources:

The various sources of published data are:

1. Reports and official publications of

    (i)   International bodies such as the International Monetary Fund, International Finance Corporation and United Nations Organisation.

    (ii) Central and State Governments such as the Report of the Tandon Committee and Pay Commission.

2. Semi-official publication of various local bodies such as Municipal Corporations and District Boards.

3. Private publications-such as the publications of –

    (i) Trade and professional bodies such as the Federation of Indian Chambers of Commerce and Institute of Chartered Accountants.

    (ii) Financial and economic journals such as 'Commerce', 'Capital' and Indian Finance'.

    (iii) Annual reports of joint stock companies.

    (iv) Publications brought out by research agencies, research scholars, etc.

2. Unpublished Sources:

All statistical material is not always published. There are various sources of unpublished data such as records maintained by various Government and private offices, studies made by research institutions, scholars, etc. Such sources can also be used where necessary.

Precautions in the use of Secondary data:

The following are some of the points that are to be considered in the use of secondary data

1. How the data has been collected and processed
2. The accuracy of the data
3. How far the data has been summarized
4. How comparable the data is with other tabulations
5. How to interpret the data, especially when figures collected for one purpose is used for Another.

Merits and Demerits of Secondary Data:

1. Secondary data is cheap to obtain. Many government publications are relatively cheap and libraries stock quantities of secondary data produced by the government, by companies and other organisations.
2. Large quantities of secondary data can be got through internet.
3. Much of the secondary data available has been collected for many years and therefore it can be used to plot trends.
4. Secondary data is of value to:

    •   The government – help in making decisions and planning future policy.

    •   Business and industry – in areas such as marketing, and sales in order to appreciate the general economic and social conditions and to provide information on competitors.

    •   Research organisations – by providing social, conomical and industrial information.

3. Primary Data

Data collection forms integral part of any research there are different ways and means of collecting data for marketing, finance, human resource related research or project the method of data collection differs. The following are the different types of primary data collection.

3.1 Primary data:

Primary data is the one, which is collected by the investigator himself for the purpose of a specific inquiry or study. Such data is original in character and is generated by survey conducted by individuals or research institution or any organization.

Example 1:

If a researcher is interested to know the impact of noon-meal scheme for the school children, he has to undertake a survey and collect data on the opinion of parents and children by asking relevant questions. Such a data collected for the purpose is called primary data.

3.2 Methods of collecting primary data / tools for collecting primary data.

The primary data can be collected by the following methods:

1. Questionnaire Method
2. Interviews Method
3. Observation Method
4. Group discussion Method

3.2.1. Questionnaire Method

Questionnaire enlists questions, which translate the research objectives into specific questions. The major issues on which questions may be concerned are facts, opinions, attitudes, respondents' motivation, and their level of acquaintance with a research problem. By and large, questions can be classified into two general categories, namely,

1. Factual questions and
2. Opinion and Attitude questions.

Factual Questions

Factual questions are asked to elicit information from the respondents regarding their background, such as sex, age, marital status, education or income. The following is an example of such a question:

Example 2:

What is your level of education?

1. Graduate ( )   2. Intermediate ( )   3. High School ( )   4. Middle School ( )

Opinion and Attitude Questions

The concept "attitude" refers to the sum total of a person's inclination, prejudices, ideas, fears, and convictions about any specific topic. Opinions, on the other hand, are the verbal expression of attitudes. Thus, a statement such as "Child labour should be banned" would reflect an opinion that is against child labour, but an attitude towards child labour would mean a more specific orientation of what a person feels and thinks about child labour.

Formats of Questions

The format of the question and the response categories accompanying the questions are other aspects, which need attention of the researchers. Three types of question formats are discussed in the following sections:

> (1) open-ended questions
>
> (2) closed-ended questions and
>
> (3) contingency questions

(1) Open-Ended Questions

An open-ended question is a question that cannot be answered with a "yes" or "no" response, or with a static response. These are phrased as a statement which requires a response. The response can be compared to information that is already known to the questioner.

(2) Closed-Ended Questions

In a closed-ended question, respondents are offered a set of answers from which they are asked to choose the one that most closely represents their views. For example, to measure sex discrimination against women in the unorganised sector, the following closed-ended question can be asked:

"Equal remuneration should be given to men and women for same work or work of similar nature."

> Strongly Agree   Agree   Undecided   Disagree   Strongly Disagree

(2) Contingency Questions

Frequently questions that are relevant to some respondents may be irrelevant to others. For example, the question **"Check the most important reasons why you are not going to college"** obviously applies only to those intermediate students who are not planning to go to college at all. It is often necessary to include questions that might apply only to some respondents and not to others. Some questions may be relevant only to females and not to males: others will only apply to respondents who are self-employed, and so on.

When a question is applicable to only a sub - group of the sample it is known as contingency question. A contingency question is a special case of a closed-ended question and it is one that applies only to a subgroup of respondents.

The relevance of the question to this subgroup is determined by the answer of respondents to a preceding question. For example, in a research study the preceding question was, **"Are you aware of the Right to the Information Act?"** The contingency question could be, **"If yes, what do you know about it?"** The relevance of the second question to the respondent is contingent upon his or her response to the preceding question. Only respondents who responded "Yes" to the preceding question will find the contingency question relevant.

Therefore, the response categories of the preceding questions will be

1. Yes (answer the following question)

2. No (skip to question 3).

Response Format

The general format is to present all possible responses and have the respondent check the appropriate response. The respondent can either encircle his or her answer or check a box or a blank as in the following examples:

"What is your marital status?

Married   ☐ Married   1. Married

Matrix Questions

The matrix question is a method for organizing a set of questions that have the same response patterns. The following is an example of matrix questions.

"In my work place the following welfare services are provided."

	<u>Yes</u>	<u>No</u>	If yes then what do you think about it?		
			Satis- factory	Fairly Satisfactory	Unsatisfactory
Crèches and Day Nurseries	( )	( )	( )	( )	( )

Sequence of Questions

Once the format of questions is decided, a researcher has to consider the order in which questions are to be placed in the questionnaire. Two general patterns of question sequence have been found to be most appropriate for motivating respondents to cooperate: the **funnel sequence and the inverted funnel sequence.**

It should be kept in mind that questions that are presented first in the questionnaire should put the respondent at ease; and if an interviewer is present; they should help in creating rapport between the researcher and the respondent. Thus, the question in the beginning should be easy to answer, interesting, and it should not deal with sensitive issues.

For example, questions about drinking habit or sex life of respondents, if placed at the beginning, in all possibilities will demotivate the respondents to answer the subsequent questions. It is also suggested that such questions be placed later, for they reduce the respondent's initial motivation to cooperate.

Questions to be Avoided

Leading Questions

A question worded in such a manner that it appears to the respondent that the researcher expects a certain answer, is commonly known as leading question. A question designed to elicit general opinion about work satisfaction might read, "How do you feel about your work?" The same question worded in a leading form might read, "Are you satisfied with your work?" This question makes it easier for respondents to answer *yes* than *no*. In answering *yes*, they are agreeing with the words of the question and are not contradicting the researcher.

As far as possible leading questions are to be avoided if one is looking for objective responses. In some situations, particularly, where leading questions may serve the research objective, leading questions with suitable wordings are used with extra care.

Threatening Questions

Threatening questions refer to behaviours that are illegal or contra-normative or behaviours that are socially deviant and are not discussed in public. For example, questions that inquire about the respondent's gambling habits, about their drinking habits, child abuse or sexual behaviours are referred as threatening questions. Often it is necessary to include such questions in studies, which the respondent may find embarrassing and thus difficult to answer.

Though it is suggested to avoid threatening questions as far as possible, in cases where it is necessary to include such questions it is advised to use a long introduction to the question (or may be indirect question) rather than asking short questions (or direct questions); by an open-ended rather than a closed-ended format; and, to a lesser extent, by letting the respondents pick their own words to talk about the sensitive issues. For example, to know about respondent's drinking behaviour the following question may be asked:

"In the past one year, how often you could not control yourself to become intoxicated while drinking?"

Respondents may be asked to classify their responses into one of the following categories: Once in three month/Once a month/Once a week/ Several times a week/ Daily

Double-barreled Questions

When two or more than two questions are included in one question it is termed as double-barreled questions. The following question is an example:

"Women should stay at home and take care of their children and other family members and stop taking up employment outside."

The above statement includes two separate questions that are joined by the conjunction 'and'. Such questions might confuse respondents who agree with one aspect of the question – stay at home and take care of children and other family members and not with the other – stop taking employment outside. Many questions that includes 'and' is very likely doubled-barreled, hence, it is suggested not to include such questions.

Instructions

While constructing a questionnaire it is utmost necessary that the instructions must go with each question or with a set of questions. Instructions are required to all such questions that are not self-explanatory. It may be general instruction such as "circle the appropriate category" or very specific instructions that explain how to rank order a set of priorities. The instructions are usually written for the interviewer and thus are often short and concise.

Basic Rules

- **KISS** Keep It Short And Simple
- **Appearance** is crucial and affects:
  - Response rate
  - Ease of data summarisation and analysis
- **Length** of questionnaire: shorter response rates
- **Question order** is important:
  - Easy to difficult
  - General to particular
  - Factual to abstract
  - Start with closed format questions.
  - Start with questions relevant to the main subject.

3.2.2. Interviews Method

The interview is a verbal interaction between the researcher and the respondents. This method has been a widely used method of data collection. This method involves presentation of verbal questions orally and collecting oral verbal responses. Many feel that the best way to find out why people behave as they do is to question them about their behaviour directly by interviewing them. In this method, the interviewer asks questions in a face-to-face contact (generally) to the interviewee, the person who is being interviewed who gives answers (mostly) to these questions.

Types of Interview

- Interview has been classified in different ways. One way of classification of interviews is based on their functions, such as diagnostic interviews often used for clinical purposes. The other way of classification of interviews is the number of persons participating in the interview process, for example, individual interview or group interviews. Yet another basis of classifying interviews is the format used for interview, for example, structured and non-structured. Any one of the bases can be relied on to classify the various types of interviews just mentioned above. Most probably, the easiest and most convenient way to classify them is the degree to which they are structured.
- The Structured Interviews
- As the name suggests, structured interviews maintain some control over the respondents. Nevertheless, considerable flexibility is permitted in deciding the extent to which interviews should be structured. First and foremost area, through which an interview is structured, is the questions and its responses. The questions in an interview are regulated to get appropriate responses. In so far as responses are concerned they are regulated and controlled by giving multiple choices to the

interviewee. To achieve this, first the questions have to be in order and help to get reliable and appropriate responses; it is beneficial to ask questions in same order from one interview to another interview.

- The Unstructured Interviews.

- In unstructured interviews questions are not ordered in a particular way. The order of questions is not fixed. In other words the order of questions followed in one interview may not be followed in the next interview. Even the questions asked are not worded in the same way. In sum, the interview is free of regulation and control.

3.2.3. Observation Method

Observation is the basic method of obtaining information about a phenomena under investigation. All of us are constantly engaged in observation. However, all such observations are not scientific observations. Observations become a method of data collection when it is planned in accordance with the purpose of research and recorded systematically keeping in mind the validity and reliability of observed data.

There are several types of observations varying from completely unstructured to structured, pre-coded, formal procedures to suit the needs of researchers and the overall objectives of the research problems. One way of differentiating among various types of observations is to draw distinction on the basis of degree of structuredness. Accordingly, we get two observational procedures:

(1) unstructured and

(2) structured.

The other way of classifications is in terms of the role played by the researcher. On this basis observation procedures may be classified as

(1) participant observation and

(2) non-participant observation.

Structured Observation

Structured observations take into consideration a clear and specific definition of the units to be observed and data to be recorded. This is possible only when the problem is well formulated. However, in exploratory studies the researcher does not know in advance which dimension of the problem will be relevant. Structured observations are mostly used in studies designed to describe a problem or to test causal hypothesis. The use of structured observation procedures presupposes that the researcher knows what aspects of the problem under study are relevant to his research objectives and is in a position therefore to plan the recording of observations before he starts data collection.

Unstructured Observations

In a practical situation it is often not possible to plan out the 'observation' process in advance. Particularly in case of exploratory studies, the researcher does not have enough clues to structure his observations, which may call for changes in what he observes. Such changes are characteristics of unstructured observation. Since the unstructured observations are flexible it allows for changes in the focus from time to time if and when reasonable clues warrant such changes.

Participant Observations

Participant observation involves sharing the life of the group under study by the researcher. In other words, participant observation is an attempt to put both the observer and the observed on the same side by making the observer a member of the group so that he can experience what they experience and work within their frame of reference. In particular, the researcher becomes a member of the community being observed by him.

Non-participant Observations

On the contrary, non-participant observation is characterised by a lack of participation by the observer in the life of the group that a researcher is observing. In other words, in non-participant observations the observer has detached role and records without any attempt on his part to participate in the interaction process with the group being observed.

3.2.4. Group discussion Method

A group discussion involving a number of people with shared experiences or characteristics that a researcher brings together for the purpose of obtaining ideas about a research topic.

Merits and Demerits of primary data:

1. The collection of data by the method of personal survey is possible only if the area covered by the investigator is small. Collection of data by sending the enumerator is bound to be expensive. Care should be taken twice that the enumerator record correct information provided by the informants.

2. Collection of primary data by framing a schedule or distributing and collecting questionnaires by post is less expensive and can be completed in shorter time.

3. Suppose the questions are embarrassing or of complicated nature or the questions probe into personnel affairs of individuals, then the schedules may not be filled with accurate and correct information and hence this method is unsuitable.

4. The information collected for primary data is mere reliable than those collected from the secondary data.

Sampling

Sometimes it is not feasible to study a whole group or an extremely large group. For example, researchers might be interested in learning about the mentally challenged children, mentally ill, prison inmates, street children or some other large group of people. It would be difficult rather impossible to study all members of these groups. Here comes a process called sampling which allows us to study a manageable number of people from the large group to derive inferences that are likely to be applicable to all the people of the large group.

Another reason why we should study a sample is, the results obtained from a sample are more precise and correct than the results from the study of the whole group. Costs involved in studying all units of a large group are yet another factor which suggests us to study a small group of people instead. Associated with cost, there are certain other factors such as time available for the study and accessibility of the units of study. Above all, the point to be kept in mind is, if we can get almost same results by studying a carefully selected small group of people why should we study the large group at all.

A single unit of study is referred to as an element of population. When we select a group of elements for the purpose of study of a particular phenomenon, we refer to that group of elements as a sample. The aggregate of all the elements that conform to some defined set of definitions is called population.

Probability and Non-Probability Sampling

The "chance"of being included in the sample is commonly known as probability. The probability of an element to be included in a sample can be ascertained on the basis of the theories of probability. The basic difference in sampling methods is between probability and non -probability sampling. The essential characteristic of sampling is that one can specify for each element of the population the chance of being included in the sample.   In non-probability sampling, there is no way of estimating the probability that each element has of being included in the sample and no assurance that every element has some chance of being included.

Probability Sampling

Major types of probability sampling are: simple random sampling stratified random sampling and cluster sampling.

Simple Random Sampling

A process that gives each element in the population an equal chance of being included in the sample is termed as simple random sampling. The elements are selected, using a list of random numbers appended with most textbooks of research and statistics. Before using the table of random numbers, it is first necessary to number all the elements in the population to be studied. Then the table is marked at some point and the cases whose numbers come up as one from this point down the column of numbers are taken into the sample until the desired number of elements is obtained. The selection of any given element places no limits on other element being selected, thus making equally possible the selection of any one of the many possible combinations of elements.

Proportionate Stratified Random Sampling

In stratified random sampling, the population is first divided into strata. The strata may be based on a single criterion or on a combination of two or more criteria. In stratified random sampling, a simple random sample is taken from each stratum, and the sub samples are then joined to form the total sample.

Disproportionate Stratified Random Sampling

This sampling plan is almost similar to proportionate stratified random sampling except that the sub samples are not necessarily distributed according to their proportionate weight in the population from which they were drawn. It is possible that some sub samples are over represented while other sub groups are under represented.

If the researcher wants to draw a disproportionate stratified random sample of 60 from this population, stratified by sex, then he has to draw 30 from each substratum, this means male students (30) will be under- represented and female students (30) will be over represented in the sample. In other words, disproportionate sampling gives equal weights to each substratum.

Cluster Sampling

In case the area of study is markedly wide spread, large expenses are involved if simple and stratified random sampling are used. For example, in the preparation of sampling frame from the population and in covering the wide spread areas by interviewers a large amount of expenditure is required. The more widely spread the area of study, the greater are the travel expenses, the greater is the time spent in traveling, and hence expensive-and the tasks of administering, monitoring and supervision of the research project and in particular supervising the field staff become more complicated. For the reasons mentioned above and few other reasons, large-scale research studies make use of the methods of cluster sampling.

In cluster sampling, first the whole research area is divided into sub area, more commonly known as "clusters". The simple random or stratified method is used to select clusters. Finally, researcher arrives at the ultimate sample size to be studied by selecting sample from within the clusters which is carried out on a simple or stratified random sampling basis.

Characteristically, the procedure moves through a series of stages-hence the common term, "multistage" sampling-from more inclusive to less inclusive sampling units until we finally arrive at the population elements that constitute the desired sample.

Non-probability Sampling

The four important types of non-probability sampling are accidental sampling, quota sampling, snowball sampling and purposive sampling.

Accidental Sampling

Accidental sampling refers to a method of selecting respondents who happen to meet the researcher and are willing to be interviewed. Thus, a researcher may take the first hundred people he meets who are willing to be interviewed.

For example, let us consider the situations where a programme director, wishes to make some generalisation about the programme in progress, selects beneficiaries who have come to the agency for a service or a community organiser, trying to know how "the people" feel about health status in that community, interviews available community dwellers like shop-keepers, daily wage earners, barbers and others who are presumed to reflect public opinion. In both the situations those who are available for study are included in the samples. This is exactly what we call accidental sampling.

Quota Sampling

Quota sampling insures inclusion of diverse elements of the population in the sample and make sure that these diverse elements take account of the proportions in which they occur in the population. For example, we take a sample from a population with equal number of boys and girls, and that there is a difference between the two groups in the characteristic we wish to study and we fail to interview any girls, the results of the study would almost certainly be extremely misleading generalisations about the population. In practice, elements in small numbers are frequently underrepresented in accidental samples. In anticipation of such possible exclusion of small groups, quota sampling ensures inclusion of enough cases from each stratum in the sample. It should be noted here that the major goal of quota sampling is the selection of a sample that is a replica of the population to which one wants to generalize.

Purposive Sampling

Purposive sampling is based on the presumption that with good judgment one can select the sample units that are satisfactory in relation to one's requirements. A common strategy of this sampling technique is to select cases that are judged to be typical of the population, in which one is interested, assuming that errors of judgment in the selection will tend to counterbalance each other.

4. Data Processing and Analysis

Data processing and analysis should start in the field, with checking for completeness of the data and performing quality control checks, while sorting the data by instrument used and by group of informants. Data of small samples may even be processed and analyzed as soon as it is collected.

Preparation of a plan for data processing and analysis will provide you with better insight into the feasibility of the analysis to be performed as well as the resources that are required. It also provides an important review of the appropriateness of the data collection tools for collecting the data you need. That is why you have to plan for data analysis before the pre-test. When you process and analyse the data you collect during the pre-test you will spot gaps and overlaps which require changes in the data collection tools before it is too late!

4.1 Data Processing

Data processing refers to certain operations such as editing, coding, computing of the scores, preparation of master charts, etc. After collection of filled in questionnaires, editing of entries therein are not only necessary but also useful in making subsequent steps simpler. Many a times, a researcher or the assistants either miss entries in the questionnaires or enter responses, which are not legible. This sort of discrepancies can be resolved by editing the schedule meticulously. Another problem comes up at the time of tabulation of data when researcher asks for tabulation of responses from consecutive questions. In cases where data are not cleaned there has to be inconsistency in the tabulations, the researcher has to be very particular about, consecutive questions where category 'not applicable' exists. In the process of editing, he has to be very careful about consecutive questions having 'not applicable' as a response.

4.1.1 Editing

The basic purpose of editing is to secure a quality standard for the data. Editing involves inspection, and if necessary, correction of questionnaire or observation forms. For example, careful editing of a questionnaire will sometimes show that an answer to question is obviously incorrect. How the questionnaire is completed may reflect whether the respondent has really read and taken the task of answering the questionnaire seriously.

4.1.2 Coding of Data

Coding of data involves assigning of numerical to each response of the question. The purpose of giving numerical symbols is to translate raw data into numerical data, which may be counted and tabulated. The task of researcher is to give numbers to response carefully.

CODE BOOK

Q.No	Var. No.	Information Sought	Responses	Code
2	1	Age	Actual	-
3	2	Designation	Worker	1
			Supervisor	2
			Manager	3
4	3	Establishment	Public	1
			Private	2
5	4	Level of Education	Graduate	1
			Intermediate	2
			High School	3
			Middle School	4
			Primary	5
			Illiterate	6
			Other	7
6	5	Marital Status	Married	1
			Unmarried	2
			Widow	3
			Divorce	4

Preparing a Master Chart

After a codebook is prepared, the data can be transferred either to a master chart or directly to computer through a statistical package. Going through master chart to computer is much more advantageous than entering data directly to computers because one can check the wrong entries in the computer by comparing 'data listing' as a computer out–put and master chart.

Entering data directly to computer is disadvantageous, as there is no way to check wrong entries, which will show inconsistencies in tabulated data at the later stages of tabulation. A sample of master chart prepared in accordance with the code- book is presented below:

MASTER CHART

VARIABLE LABELS

AGE	DESIGNATION	ESTABLISHMENT	LEVEL OF EDUCATION	MARITAL STATUS	NATURE OF WORK	DURATION OF WORK	WAGES	PROMOTIONS	ATTITUDE OF EMPLOYER
V1	V2	V3	V4	V5	V6	V7	V8	V9	V10
24	1	2	1	2	3	2	3	4	3
21	2	3	4	5	6	7	8	9	5
23	3	3	4	2	6	7	2	6	2
25	7	8	9	1	3	5	6	1	1
24	5	1	4	2	1	1	4	3	3
23	1	2	3	4	5	6	3	1	5
25	4	5	6	9	7	8	5	2	4
21	4	2	5	3	6	3	7	8	9
22	2	4	2	6	7	8	2	1	5
29	5	6	8	7	9	2	4	4	3
22	2	8	4	9	3	4	7	3	8
22	5	7	9	5	1	4	2	4	3
22	9	4	5	6	7	2	6	9	6
22	8	7	9	5	2	4	6	2	3
23	5	4	8	7	9	2	4	2	3
22	4	8	7	9	5	8	4	5	6
28	7	4	9	4	3	4	6	3	4

The row "V1 ... V10" above is labelled **VARIABLE NUMBER** on the page.

Data Analysis

The purpose of data analysis is to prepare data as a model where relationships between the variables can be studied. Analysis of data is made with reference to the objectives of the study and research questions if any. It is also designed to test the hypothesis.

Univariate Analysis

Univariate analysis refers to tables, which gives data relating to one variable. Uni-variate tables, which are more commonly known as frequency distribution tables, show how frequently an item repeats. Example of a frequency table is given below.

PHYSICAL AND PSYCHOLOGICAL HEALTH OF RESPONDENTS

Physical and Psychological health	Distribution of Respondents	
	Frequencies	Percentages
High	110	38.6
Medium	107	37.5
Low	68	23.9
Total	**285**	**100.0**

Bivariate Analysis

Once we describe the independent and dependent variable, we look for bivariate associations among the variables. A bivariate table presents data of two variables with row or column percentages. Bivariate tables with row percentages are shown below:

PHYSICAL AND PSYCHOLOGICAL HEALTH AND LIFE SATISFACTION

Physical and Psychological health	Life Satisfaction			Total
	High	Medium	Low	
High	37(33.6)	63 (57.3)	10 (9.1)	110 (100.0)
Medium	22(20.6)	56 (52.3)	29 (27.1)	107 (100.0)
Low	1 (1.5)	23 (33.8)	44 (64.7)	68 (100.0)
Total	60(21.1)	142 (49.8)	83 (29.1)	285 (100.0)

$\chi^2 = 70.397$ $\qquad$ df = 4 $\qquad$ p = ˙000 significant $\qquad$ C = 0.445

The association between two variables can be explained either by comparing the percentages of respondent's column wise or row wise depending upon computation of percentages. If the percentages are calculated row wise, we compare data column wise. The association between the variables can also be examined by various statistical techniques depending upon the level of measurement of the data. Since the data are in nominal levels of measurement the Chi-square test would be more appropriate in this case. Apparently, associations between independent variables and the dependent variable – life satisfaction are statistically significant and hence the variables are interdependent. Therefore, it may be inferred that while older adults with higher physical and psychological health higher level of life satisfaction.

Trivariate Analysis

Trivariate and multivariate analyses serve three important functions in research; control, elaboration and prediction. Firstly, whenever the experimental control is not possible, trivariate analysis is used to examine the bivariate relationship to see if the relationship is due to the third variable. Secondly, bivariate relationship is clarified by introducing a third variable. Finally, trivariate analysis helps to identify more independent variables to account for the variation in the dependent variable.

Cross Tabulation as a Method of Control

In this method the sample is divided into subgroups according to the categories of the controlled variable. The variables which show an association with independent and dependent variables are selected as control variables. The original bivariate association is reexamined within each subgroup.

There are three possibilities:

(1) the original bivariate association is not affected by the third variable,

(2) the original bivariate association is affected by the third variable and the association is disappeared, and

(3) the original bivariate association is partially affected.

While, when a third variable completely accounts for the bivariate association between the independent and dependent variable the association is referred as spurious whereas if a third variable does not accounts for the bivariate association between the independent and dependent variable the association is referred as non-spurious. The results of crosstabulation of data are presented below:

PHYSICAL AND PSYCHOLOGICAL HEALTH AND LIFE SATISFACTION
(CONTROLLING FOR SPIRITUAL WELL-BEING)

Spiritual Well-Being			Life Satisfaction			
			High	Medium	Low	Total
Low	Physical and Psychological Health	High	3 (75.0)	11 (32.4)	3 (8.3)	17 (23.0)
		Medium	1 (25.0)	13 (38.2)	8 (22.2)	22 (29.7)
		Low	0 (0.0)	10 (29.4)	25 (69.4)	35 (47.3)
Total			4 (100.0)	34 (100.0)	36 (100.0)	74 (100.0)
χ^2=8.83 df =4			P = ˙001	Significant	C=.45	
Medium	Physical and Psychological Health	High	21 (58.3)	30 (42.3)	5 (12.5)	56 (38.1)
		Medium	14 (38.9)	30 (42.3)	19 (47.5)	63 (42.9)
		Low	1 (2.8)	11 (15.5)	16 (40.0)	28 (19.0)
		Total	36 (100.0)	71 (100.0)	40 (100.0)	147(100.0)
χ^2 =26.104		df =4			p = ˙000 significant c=.38	
High	Physical and Psychological Health	High	13 (65.0)	22 (59.5)	2 (28.6)	37 (57.8)
		Medium	7 (35.0)	13 (35.1)	2 (28.6)	22 (34.4)
		Low	0 (0.0)	2 (5.4)	3 (42.9)	5 (7.8)
		Total	20 (100.0)	37 (100.0)	7 (100.0)	64 (100.0)
χ^2 =14.149		df =4			p = ˙007 significant c=.42	

In the last table, it is observed that the original bivariate association remains unaffected by the third variable-'spiritual well being'. In the total sample as well as in each subgroup of 'spiritual wellbeing' the proportion of 'life satisfaction' is unchanged. The result shows that the original bivariate association between the two variables is not accounted for by the control variable 'spiritual wellbeing'.

Thus, it may be concluded that 'spiritual wellbeing' has no effect on the association between 'physical and psychological health' and 'life satisfaction'. In other words, we can infer that the association between 'physical and psychological health' (independent variable) and 'life satisfaction' (dependent variable) is ***non-spurious***.

Partial Correlation as a Method of Control

An alternative method of control is the partial correlation. This is a mathematical process of adjustment of the bivariate correlation, deemed to nullify the effect of third variable (control variable) on the independent and dependent variables.

Multivariate Analysis

Often, we have situations where a set of independent variables is associated with dependent variable. In other words, more often several independent variables contribute to the prediction of the dependent variable. Multiple Regression is commonly used to estimate the effect of multiple independent variables.

4.1.3 Measurement in Research

Concept of Measurement

The concept of measurement refers to the process of describing abstract concepts in terms of specific indicators by assigning numbers to these indicants in accordance with rules. In marketing research, measurement has become an essential prerequisite because of a number of reasons. One of the important reasons is to allow the researcher the opportunity of using variables in hypotheses to determine the effects of a set of variables on others.

Consider the following, questions?

1.   Do you save money? Yes/No

2.   If yes, how much? Rs……..

3.   "Child labour in our country must be banned".

Strongly Agree   Agree   Undecided   Disagree   Strongly Disagree

The three questions attempt to measure some of the aspects of street children. The first question measures one aspect by determining the presence or absence of a characteristic 'saving habit' among street children.

The second question tries to measure in a more specific way involving the amount saved which tries to determine the degree of intensity of saving. Finally, a reaction or comment to a statement is in a sequence of responses, which in turn can be converted into scores and would measure the phenomena in question more specifically.

Levels of Measurement

Levels of measurement refer to a set of rules that define permissible mathematical functions that can be performed on numbers/scores produced by a measure. There are four levels of measurement, namely; nominal, ordinal, interval and ratio.

Nominal Level of Measurement

Nominal level of measurement is the lowest and most simple level of measurement. When a variable is classified into nominal subclasses it is said that the variable in question is measured on a nominal level. For example, the variable, sex, has two nominal subclasses, male and female. Similarly, religions have many subclasses, if not infinite, among which are included Hindu, Muslim, Christian and Sikhs. Numbers assigned to nominal subclasses at this level of measurement represent serial order only. The numbers do not have mathematical values. Hence no mathematical function is or possible with nominal data.

Ordinal Level of Measurement

When the relative positions of objects or persons with respect to some characteristics are defined, measurements are possible on ordinal levels. The fundamental requirement of an ordinal level of measurement is that one be able to determine the order of positions of objects or persons in terms of characteristics under study. Ordinal level measurements are considered of higher level than nominal level because in addition to being mutually exclusive (feature of nominal level of measurement) the categories have a fixed order. Level of education, for example, constitutes an ordinal variable and measures levels of education on ordinal scales.

Interval Level of Measurement

Interval level between the categories of measurement have equal spacing in addition to the characteristics of nominal level (mutually exclusive) and ordinal level (having fixed order). In interval measures the positions are not only ordered either in ascending order (lower, middle and higher) or in descending order (higher, middle and lower) but the intervals of measurement are also equal.

In other words, the distance between the positions is equal, such as the degrees of a temperature scales. The examples of true interval scales are Fahrenheit and Celsius temperature scales. The units of measurement of both the scales are degree and are based on equal spacing characteristics of interval level of measurement.

Ratio Level of Measurement

For example, income can be measured at ratio level of measurement because it has an absolute zero (no income, at least in money terms, not in term of economic status). Hence, a person with monthly income of Rs. 15,00-00 has thrice as much as a person earning Rs. 500-00. Most of the function can be performed on data measurement on interval scales.

Scaling Techniques

Likerts's Scales:

Six Steps in the Construction of a Likert Scale :
1. Compiling possible scale items
2. Administering items to a random sample respondents
3. Computing a total score for each respondent
4. Determining the discriminative power of items
5. Selecting the scale items, and
6. Testing reliability.

Thurstone Scales:

This scaling technique involves five steps:
1. Compiling scale items,
2. Asking judges to order them,
3. Computing average value for each item,
4. Selecting the specific scale items and computing the cumulative   percentage values, and
5. Testing the relevancy of the items.

4.2 Hypothesis & its testing

Once we have formulated the problem for research, we proceed to formulate tentative solutions or answers to it. These proposed answers or solutions constitute the hypothesis, that we need to test on the basis of facts, which is to be collected in the course of our research study. Thus, the term hypothesis can be defined as a proposition or tentative solutions or answers or generalisations, which are yet to be tested.

Sources of Hypothesis

Available literature is considered as the major source of hypothesis. While reviewing the literature a researcher comes across various theories and assumptions. These theories and assumptions form the bases of several hypotheses. Personal experiences, the socialisation process and learning experiences are some other sources of hypothesis. On the basis of personal experiences a researchers may be able to generate hypothesis. Many a times views peculiar to persons and causal observations help a researcher to formulate hypotheses.

Findings of other study are often a source of valuable hypotheses. A researcher on the basis of the findings of other studies may hypothesise that the similar causal relationship between a set of variables will hold good in his present study too.

Some Characteristics of Usable Hypothesis

The chief characteristic of a usable hypothesis is it must be empirically testable. This means when a researcher formulates his hypothesis he must be aware of the instruments available to measure the variables included in the hypothesis. This is also because of the fact that unless a researcher is aware of the available tools for measurement he will not be able to test his hypothesis empirically. Conversely, hypotheses must not be moral judgments because it would be impracticable to measure the variables in the hypotheses. Finally, hypotheses are required to be conceptually clear and as far as possible specific.

Research Hypotheses (H$_1$)

The hypothesis derived from theories is termed as research hypothesis or working hypothesis. The researcher, who wishes to study a phenomenon, looks for various theories about the phenomenon, because theories explain the nature of things or events.

Thus, these explanations are regarded as suppositions or tentative statements about reality until they are verified to the researcher's satisfaction. These suppositions or statements identified by the researchers for testing are known as research hypothesis and conventionally symbolised as H$_1$.

Examples of research hypotheses are:

1.   Personal and socio-economic variables may be associated with organizational effectiveness.
2.   It is likely that organizational culture, productivity, leadership styles and organizational effectiveness are interdependent.

5. Writing Skills for Business Research

The research task is not completed until the report has been written. It is an indispensable task of any research and empirical study. The objective is to record the process and findings for implementation and further reference and the outcomes could have important impact on the development of theory. Communicating the results so that they become part of the general store of knowledge is an essential part of the researcher's responsibilities which should deserve the same attention that earlier stages do.

The most important point to be kept in mind when initiating the process of writing the report is its function. Reporting of a research study depends on its purposes as all research reports vary in *their* purposes. The manner in which the research findings will be disseminated should guide the design of the project through out. Before writing the research report these four basic ingredients must be assembled.

5.1 Organizing a Research Report

The components of a research report consist of the preliminaries, the main body and the supplementary.

The Preliminaries	The Text	The Reference aterial
Title Page	Introduction	Bibliography/References
Acknowledgements	Review of Literature	Appendices
Contents	Research Methodology	
List of Tables	Analysis and Interpretation of Data	
List of Figures	Major Findings and Conclusions	

The following outline should be able to be applicable to nearly all types of research methods /approaches.

i.   **General Statement of the Research Problem:** The statement of the research problem must state clearly and concisely what the problem is, and what the general issue is that the study will address. The general problem must be stated in such a way that the design of the study, the data collection, and the analyses make logical sense as a way to address the problem.

ii.   **Background of the Problem:** Research problems grow forms the ideas and findings of earlier studies, earlier observations of what the researcher is studying. Therefore, the earlier findings must *be* presented. This is the background *literature or review of the literature section.* Understanding clearly what the primary focus of the study is helps in finding out the most central and important studies and theories, which have laid the ground, work for the present study.

iii.   **Design of the study:** *T*his is where the formal statement of the specific research question or hypothesis is made. Generally, the researcher draws on the ideas that are introduced in the statement of the problem and on the background literature. The report should build on the section 1 and 2 and lead to section 3 where the problem, which is being addressed, is explicitly laid out. The type of study focused the primary dependent and independent variables selected will be determined from the research question and hypothesis formulated. The major concepts should be defined theoretically and explained operationally.

iv.   **How the data were obtained:**   This is the section of the report that includes how the researcher did the study. It is the central methods section. There are two primary aspects to it: The first is what the researcher did to get the data (Data Collection) and the second is from whom the data was collected (The Sample).

v.   **Analysis of Data:**   This is the heart of the report. This section is a result of the introductory material in the earlier section, the reasons for the analysis and an understanding of what the data represent. All facts must be interpreted and it is the choice of interpretations that will form the basis of the analysis. In quantitative studies the analysis of the data includes tables in it.

vi.   **Discussion:** Once the facts and finding are presented there is a need to discuss them in more general terms relating to what the expectations of the researcher were when the study was designed. In other words, the discussion should relate the empirical findings to the past and to the theory. In case a hypothesis is not proven it can be discussed as to why this might be the case. The researcher can relate major findings to those of others mentioned in the review of literature. It should also be clarified as to what is important and specific about the study. It can also give certain areas of findings that might be profitably used by other researchers.

vii.   **Conclusion:**   Conclusions relating to the findings should be made in this section. Conclusions are generally made on the basis of the statistical accuracy of the findings got and the relevance to the population under study. The conclusion should include the researcher's views of the research process and findings and the implications of the study for further experimentation.

Writing Research Report

Communicating the results so that they become part of the general store of knowledge is an essential part of the researcher's responsibilities which should deserve the same attention that earlier stages do.

Organizing A Research Report

TITLE PAGE

- Title of the report
- Name of the Research Scholar
- Degree for which the report is presented
- Name of the Faculty / Department
- Name of the Institution
- Month and Year of Submission

SAMPLE TITLE PAGE OF A THESIS

A STUDY OF ORGANISATIONAL CULTURE AND ITS EFFECT ON LEADERSHIP, PRODUCTIVITY AND ORGANISATIONAL EFFECTIVENESS IN SELECT INDUSTRIES OF VARODARA

By

Ms. XYZ

Research Supervisor

Dr. ABC

Report Submitted To

M.S. University

Faculty of Business Management

For the Award of the Degree of

BBA/MBA

In Business Management

Department of Business Management

University of Pune, Pune

April 2007

SAMPLE TABLE OF CONTENTS

CONTENTS	Page
ACKNOWLEDGEMENTS	ii
LIST OF TABLES	iii
LIST OF FIGURES	iv
Chapter	
1. INTRODUCTION	23
2. REVIEW OF LITERATURE	47
3. RESEARCH METHODOLOGY	87
Research Design	91
4. DATA INTERPRETATION AND ANALYSIS	121
5. MAJOR FINDINGS AND CONCLUSIONS	134
BIBLIOGRAPHY	231
APPENDIXES	235

SAMPLE LIST OF TABLES

LIST OF TABLES

Table	Page
1. Age of Respondents	12
2. Marital Status	15
3. Monthly Income	23

PAGE AND CHAPTER FORMAT

Research Methodology

- Introduction
- Research Design
- Population and Sample
  - Size of Sample.
- Method and Tools of Data Collection
  - Primary Data
  - Secondary Data
- Writing research report
  - Introduction
  - Review of Literature

- Research Methodology
- Profile of the Respondents
- Analysis and Interpretation of Data
- Main Findings and Conclusions

Introduction

- The Background
- Statement of The Problem
- Theoretical Framework
- Significance of the Study
- Scheme of the Report
- This section addresses the problem studied by the researcher.
- In this section researcher has to explain the purposes of the study the reason why, it is carried out.
- If it is to explore, describe or explain a problem, it must be stated in the beginning of this chapter.

It should explain the focus of the study, whether it centers on a search for the determinants of a dependent variable,

on an appraisal of a programme or condition serving as the independent variable or on a special group will be addressed.

Statement of the Problem

The statement of the research problem must state clearly and concisely what the problem is, and what the general issue is that the study will address. The general problem must be stated in such a way that the design of the study, the data collection, and the analyses make logical sense as a way to address the problem.

Review of Relevant Literature

- The background material should have been well gathered together when the research was designed.
- Most recent, articles books relevant to the topic must be carefully selected and considered for inclusion depending on their relevance and the extent of their contribution to the research.

Research Methodology

- The research methodology explains the complete process of research.
- It is primarily the model which is proposed to be used to analyse the data and includes the proposals for measuring the major variables and collection of data.
- The Problem
- Objectives of the Study
- Hypotheses
- Conceptualization
- Measurement of Variables
- Research Design
- Population and Sample

- Methods and Tools of Data Collection
- Data Processing and Analysis
- Limitations of the Study

Profile of the Respondents

- Age
- Gender
- Education
- Income
- Employment

Analysis and Interpretation of Data

1. This is the heart of the report.
2. This section is a result of the introductory material in the earlier section, the reasons for the analysis and an understanding of what the data represent.
3. All facts must be interpreted and it is the choice of interpretations that will form the basis of the analysis.
4. In quantitative studies the analysis of the data includes tables in it. The tables must be carefully planned so that, they show the readers what they need to be shown to understand the table.
5. Tables must be well labeled and must be presented in a format, which is conventionally used for that type of data.

Analysis and Interpretation of Data

1. This section needs to be highly focused.
2. The tendency to report every finding and to move from one point to the next without a clear sense of which finding are more important and more central to the purpose of the study should be avoided.
3. Even if the study does not support the hypothesis it must be reported. Negative findings can be as interesting and useful as positive ones.

Main Findings and Conclusions

1. Main findings should be presented in this section.
2. Conclusions are generally made on the basis of the statistical results.
3. The conclusion should include the researchers views based on findings and the implications of the study for further experimentation.
4. If the findings of the study do have any discrepancy in comparison with those of other researches or if the findings do not explain sufficiently the situation or problem under study or if they are inadequate for generalization, explanations with proper justification have to be provided.
5. The implications are to be clearly and categorically noted as it will become easy for the practitioners to implement them and to other research findings.

Discussion

Once the facts and finding are presented there is a need to discuss them in more general terms relating to what the expectations of the researcher were when the study was designed. In other words, the discussion should relate the empirical findings to the past and to the theory.

In case a hypothesis is not proven it can be discussed as to why this might be the case.

1. The researcher can relate major findings to those of others mentioned in the review of literature.
2. It should also be clarified as to what is important and specific about the study.
3. It can also give certain areas of findings that might be profitably used by other researchers.

References / Bibliography

- *Example:* Single Author

According to George Lundberg (1946), scientific method consists of three basic steps, systematic observation, classification and interpretation of data.

Lundberg, George (1946). *Social Research*, New York: Longman.

- *Example*: Single Author (quoting exact words of author)

Social research, then, like research in physical and natural sciences, seeks to establish, measure, analyse and these associations in all their variety and intensity (Thomas, 1968, p.294).

Thomas, P.T. (1977). "Social Research "in *Encyclopaedia of Social Work India.* New Delhi : Govt. of India. p.294.

- *Example:* Two Authors

Wilkinson, T.S. and Bhandarkar, P.L. (1977). *Methodology and Techniques of Social Research.* Bombay: Himalaya Publishing.

- *Example:* More than two Authors

Monette, Duane R. et. al. (1986). Applied Social Research: Tool For the Human Services, Chicago: Holt.

5.2 Research Paper (Sample)

Awareness of cyber crimes - India

ABSTRACT

IT Act 2000 has enforced on 17th Oct 2000 in India. The main objective of enactment of IT Act is to increase the E-commerce & decrease the cyber crimes happening in India. Out of this curiosity how many of the Indian citizens were aware about the some of the crimes like they are victim of identity theft? Have they received any threatening email or have these people harassed by email? Have the people of India cheated through email? These are the some issued raised by the researcher in this paper. The researcher has taken Advocates,

police, expert in the computer field, Businesspersons and the judges as a respondent for the consideration. Researcher has used the SPSS package for observations and conclusion of the above-mentioned topics. Parametric & non-parametric Statistics methods have been used to see the effect of IT Act and its awareness in the Society.

I.INTRODUCTION

Cyber security is a big challenge for India. The government of India is not only unaware about the basics of cyber security but is also adamant about not bringing suitable Changes.

The rajya sabha and lok sabha have acted not only hastily but also irresponsibly while passing the IT Act Amendment Bill, 2008. Surprisingly, till now the amended bill has not been made public by the government of India. It seems the government is not serious about bringing suitable changes in the IT Act, 2000 either

due to absence of expertise or due to political reasons. Whatever the reasons may be but the government has no choice but to bell the cat now.

India must appreciate that for a safe and secure cyberspace, we need a good legal framework. The present IT Act, 2000 is a piece make legislation that is weak on the fronts of cyber law, cyber security, cyber forensics, etc. In the absence of a sound legal framework for the ICT systems in India, other e-governance projects of government are also in poor state. As each component of e-governance is related to some other one, a deficiency in the basic legal and technological framework would bring sad results for India. It is high time for India to do some good work in the fields of cyber law, cyber security and cyber forensics.

Information technology (IT) has changed the way we behave and work in the present society. However, it has also raised certain law enforcement problems. Though India has enacted the IT Act, 2000 as the sole cyber law of India yet its effect is far from satisfactory. Similarly, the telecommunication laws in India are also deficient when it comes to IT security in India.

The frequent use of wireless networks by the terrorists and cyber criminals has forced the Indian Government to give a relook to the present cyber security condition of India. The Department of Telecommunications (DOT), Department of Information and Technology (DIT) and Telecom Regulatory Authority of India (TRAI) are jointly working in the direction of providing safe and secure wireless norms and regulations in India.

Further electronic surveillance has also been enhanced by India to curb the menace of cyber terrorism and cyber crimes in India. Senior officials in New Delhi who are aware of the Government's policy regarding cyber terrorism are of the opinion that effective mechanisms have been put in place to sniff and monitor the domestic Internet traffic at various points for suspected terror emails and other communication. This means that we must pay more attention towards issues like cyber security and wireless security where India needs to work effectively and constructively. We must pay special attention towards securing the wireless networks and connections. Suitable provisions must also be incorporated in the IT Act, 2000 as well.

The wireless networks are increasingly used in India. On the one hand we have the convenience of using wireless networks whereas on the other hand they are prone to hacking and other cyber crimes making them the premier crime perpetuation platform. The Information Technology Act, 2000 (IT Act, 2000) is the exclusive cyber law of India and it is silent on this aspect. We are also witnessing an increased use of insecure wireless networks for sending mails either before or after the terrorist attacks in India. This is not only framing the innocent people of India for terrorist attacks but is also creating a technological problem for the law enforcement in India. In India we have very few experts who can manage issues related to cyber law and cyber forensics.

This does not mean that we must keep our wireless systems unprotected and insecure. Wireless hacking becomes tougher if security mechanisms are at place. Otherwise even a novice person may also hack the wireless systems. India must concentrate upon stringent cyber law, robust cyber security, capable cyber forensics workforce and sound and stringent crisis management strategies for meeting terrorist attacks with an iron hand.

By considering above situation here in this study we are taking survey of the people those who have received harassing mails. After their receiving harassing mails what were their reactions about that five categories of people are the respondents for the study?

Total 323 respondents were given their view about the receiving or not receiving of harassing mails. Out of that 46 respondents said yes for receiving the harassing mail. After receiving the harassing mail what they have did is also considered in this study.

II. DATA ANALYSIS & INTERPRETATION

Table No. 1

People received Harassed Mails through Internet

Response	Frequency	Percent
Yes	46	14.2
No	274	84.8
Cant Say	2	0 6
Total	322	99.7

Table No. 1 furnishes the information about the harassed mails are received by people. 14.2% people said that they have received harassed mails through internet while 84.8 % people have not received such mails.

Table No. 2

Responses of Peoples on Harassed Mails

Peoples Response after receiving harassed mail	Total Respondents	Yes	Percent
Ignored it	46	10	21.73
Deleted the e-mails	46	27	58.69
Got a new account and changed e-mail Address	46	3	6.52
Replied to the email	46	2	4.34
Blocked the sender	46	2	4.34
Reported it to the Local Police	46	2	4.34

Table No. 2 furnishes the information about the harassed mails are received by people but they ignored it. 21.73% people said that they have received harassed mails through internet but they just ignored. The information about the harassed mails are received by people but they deleted it. 58.69% people said that they have received harassed mails through internet but they deleted it. The information about the harassed mails are received by people and got a new account and changed e-mail address. 6.52% people said that they have received harassed mails through internet and got a new account and changed e- mail address. The information about the harassed mails are received by people and they replied to it. 4.34% people said that they have received harassed mails through internet and they replied it.

The information about the harassed mails are received by people and they blocked the sender. 4.34% people said that they have received harassed mails through internet and they blocked the sender. The information about the harassed mails are received by people and they reported it to the local police. 4.34% people said that they have received harassed mails through internet and they reported it to the local police.

Table No. 3

Gender wise classification of Harassed Mails Received to the People

Sex	Yes	No	Can't Say
Male	40 (16%)	208 (83.20%)	2 (0.8%)
Female	6 (8.3%)	66 (91.6%)	0
Total	46	274	2

Table No. 3 furnishes the information about gender wise classification of harassed mails received to the people. 16% males have received the harassed e-mails while 8.3% females have received harassed e-mails.

Table No. 4

Education wise classification of Harassed Mails Received to the People

Education	Yes	No	Cant Say
Graduate	8 (9.3%)	78 (90.69%)	0
Post Graduate	31 (19.87%)	123 (78.84)	2 (1.2%)
Professional	7 (8.75%)	73 (91.25%)	0
Total	46	274	2

Table No.4 furnishes the information about education wise classification of harassed mails received to the people. 9.3% graduates have received the harassed e-mails, 19.87% post graduates have received harassed e-mails while 8.75% professional have received harassed e-mails.

Table No. 5

Age wise classification of Harassed Mails Received to the People

Age	Yes	No	Cant Say
Below 18	0	0	0
Between 18 to 36	39 (15.11%)	217 (84.10%)	2 (0.77%)
Between 37 to 54	7 (11.47%)	54 (88.52%)	0
Above 54	0	3 (100%)	0
Total	46	274	2

Table No. 5 furnishes the information about age wise classification of harassed mails received to the people. 15.11% people between 18 to 36 age group have received the harassed e-mails and 11.47% people between 37 to 54 age group have received the harassed e-mails while below 18 age and above 54 ages didn't receive harassed e-mails.

Table No. 6

Occupation wise classification of Harassed Mails Received to the People

Occupation	Yes	No	Cant Say
Judiciary	0	1 (100%)	0
Police	0	25 (100%)	0
Advocate	7 (5.73%)	115 (94.26%)	0
Business Person	2 (6.8%)	27 (93.10%)	0
Experts	37 (25.51%)	106 (73.10%)	2 (1.3%)
Total	46	274	2

Table No. 6 furnishes the information about occupation wise classification of harassed mails received to the people. 5.73 % advocates have received the harassed e-mails, 6.8% business persons have received the harassed e-mails and 25.51% experts have received harassed e-mails while judiciary and police didn't receive harassed e-mails.

III. CONCLUSION

Instead of enactment of IT Act 2000 people are receiving harassed mails and they are unable to decide what to do for such harassed mails.

Table no. 7

Peoples reaction after Receiving Harassed Mails

Deleted the e-mail	58.69%
Changed account	6.52%
Replied	4.34%
Blocked	4.34%
Police Report	4.34%
Ignored	21.73%

The above research shows that, majority of the people are deleting their harassed mails or just ignore them. Only 4.34% people reported to police. It indicates that, their is no appropriate awareness in the people of India regarding Cyber Crime. Government need to arrange seminar and increase the workshop for awareness of IT Act 2000 in the people of India.

IV. ACKNOWLEDGEMENT

We take this opportunity to express my gratitude towards Prof. M. N. Navale, Founder President of STES, Pune, for his constant encouragement and support for quality education. We would like to thank Dr. Daniel Penkar (Director - SIOM) and Dr. V. D. Nandavadekar (Director MCA - SIOM) for providing valuable guidelines to submit this paper.

V. REFERENCES:

1. G. Rathinasabapathy, Cyber Crimes and Information Frauds: EMERGING CHALLENGES FOR PROFESSIONALS, 1991-[Book]

2. Jerry Kang , University of California, Los Angeles - School of Law"Cyber-Race" , Harvard Law Review, Vol. 113, p. 1131, 2000-[Research Paper]

3. Patricia Brumfield, Compilation of Cyber Laws (A Preliminary Analysis of federal and State Electronic Commerce Laws), June 2000-[Book]

4. Abraham D. Sofaer , Seymour E. Goodman, Mariano-Florentino Cuéllar, Ekaterina A. Drozdova, David D. Elliott, Gregory D. Grove, Stephen J. Lukasik , Tonya L. Putnam ,George D. Wilson,The Hoover Institution , The Consortium for Research, August 2000-[Research Paper]

5. Neal Kumar Katyal, Georgetown University Law Center,"Criminal Law in Cyberspace ", University of Pennsylvania Law Review, Vol. 149, April 2001-[Research Paper]

6. Commander Barbara Etters ,THE FORENSIC CHALLENGES OF E-CRIME, Australasian Centre for Policing Research, PO Box 370, Marden, South Australia, 5070, AUSTRALIA, Sep 2001-[Research Paper]

7. Susan W Brenner, University of Dayton School of Law,"Cyber crime Investigation and Prosecution, April 2002-[Research Paper]

8. Devadatt Kamat Devad Kamat states in his research paper "Information Technology Act 2000 – A Contractual Perspective" Dec 2002-[Research Paper]

9. Pradeep Tomar, "New Vision of Computer Forensic Science:Need of Cyber Crime Law", Department of Computer Science & Applications ,M.D.University ,Rohtak, Haryana, India, Dec 2002-[Research Paper]

10. 10.R. Benjamin, B. Gladman and B. Randell, Protecting IT Systems from Cyber Crime Large-scale commercial, industrial and financial, Visiting Professor, Imperial College, London, University College, London, University of Bristol, June 2003-[Research Paper]

11. Talwant Singh , "Cyber Law & Information Technology", Addl. Distt. & Sessions Judge, Delhi, Jan 2004-[Research Paper]

12. Amit Nayak, Understanding Cyber Crime Movements in Asia, 2004-[Research Paper]

13. Kyung-shick Choi1, Bridgewater State College, USA,"Computer Crime Victimization and Integrated Theory: An Empirical Assessment ",April 2004-[Research Paper]

14. Dr. Farooq Ahmad,CYBER LAW IN INDIA (LAW ON INTERNET) book written by Dr. Farooq Ahmad, Reader, Department of Law, University of Kashmir, Srinagar-190006, 2004-[Research Paper]
15. 15.N.S.Abouzakhar,A Gani and G Manson, Bayesian Learning Networks, Jan 2004-[Research Paper]

16. Brian Cashell, William D. Jackson, Mark Jickling, and Baird Webel, The Economic Impact of Cyber-Attacks April 1, 2004-[Research Paper]

5.3 Communication research

Report Writing Styles:

English: The Langauge

1. English is the language of the day.
2. It is the International language.
3. We take the British English as a model.
4. Use of simple idiomatically correct English language is the trend of the day.
5. A good writer develops a respect for language, a taste for phrase and a sense of proportion, which one can learn, through constant reading.

Style of Writing

1. The style of writing a research report is different from other writings.
2. The report should be very concise, unambiguous, and creatively presented.
3. The presentation should be simple, direct and in short sentences.
4. The overriding criteria for good scientific writing are accuracy and clarity.

5. Statements made should be as precise as possible

6. They should be objective and there should be no room for subjectivity, personal bias and persuasion.

7. Similarly, over generalization must be avoid.

8. There is no place for hackneyed, slang and flippant phrases and folk expressions.

9. The writing style should be such that the sentences describe and explain the data, but do not try to convince or pursue the reader.

10. Since the report describes what has already been completed, the writing should be in the past tense.

11. In the case of citations, only the last name of the author is used, and in all cases academic and allied titles like, Dr., Prof., Mr., Mrs., Ms., etc. should be avoided.

12. The use of personal pronouns like *"I", "We"* etc., should be avoided.

Abbreviations of Words

1. Abbreviations/ Acronyms – like *HMT, BBA, BCA, NIRD, IIT, IIM etc.* should be avoided.

2. In case it is used frequently, it can be used by providing List of Abbreviations/ Acronyms (with its expansion) after List of Tables to avoid long names repeatedly inside the text, as well as in figures, tables, and footnotes.

3. Symbols in place of words should be avoided:

   ***For example*:**

   1. & in place of 'and'
   2. % in place of percentage or per cent

4. Acronym in place of words should be avoided:

   For example:

   1. i.e. in place of 'that is'
   2. e.g. in place of 'for example'

5. Special care should be taken while using quantitative terms in a report, such as "few" for number, "less" for quantity etc.

6. Single digit numbers like 1,2, 3,......,9 should be written as one, two, three,…nine.

Use of Quantitative Terms

1. No sentence should begin with numerical like "40 supervisors" , instead it should start as "Forty supervisors".

2. Commas should be used when numbers exceed three digits – 1,556 or 523,489 , etc.

Drafting and Crafting

1. Drafting and Crafting of the content is a skill by itself. Drafting the content clearly and in a logical manner can be done by using linking devices in a variety of ways, as shown below: Emphasize: certainly, indeed, surely, above all, most importantly.

2. *Add to*: in addition to, furthermore, also, moreover, too.

3. **Sum up**:to sum up, to summarize, to conclude, in about so, so far, altogether, thus, therefore, finally, lastly, at-last, briefly, in brief.

4. **Explain:** in other words, that is to say, namely, in this case, in fact, as a matter of fact, that is , moreover.

5. **Confirm**: also, more over, furthermore, in addition, again, what is more, above all.

6. **Show a contrast**: instead, in contrast, by contrast, conversely, on the contrary, on the other hand, unlike, whereas

7. **Show a concession**: however, still, yet, though, in spite of all the same, nonetheless, for all that, at the same time, it's true, that, as though, even, of course, after all.

Conventions of Spellings

Care should be taken while using the conventions of spellings e.g.

- Programme or Program
- Labour or Labor
- Favour or Favour
- Focussed or Focused
- Organisation or Organization

Punctuation

- Punctuation too plays a significant role.
- A simple change in placing of a comma can play havoc with its intended meaning.

For example:

Order given to a hangman: ***"Hang him not leave him"***

"Hang him, not leave him"

"Hang him not, leave him"

Capital Letter

1. It is used at the beginning of a sentence, for proper nouns, for abbreviations.

2. A common error in research studies is that the main concepts are often capitalized for emphasis for e.g. customer satisfaction, organisational effectiveness, price index etc.

3. When these concepts are discussed in the report, they need not start in capital letters, except for headings and sub-headings.

Quotation Marks

Quotation marks or inverted commas are used to enclose words actually spoken by the speaker or texts cited from a book / article. But many times, it is misused to enclose the concepts in the study, which is a major error. This should be avoided.

Underlining

1.   Underlining certain phrases or concepts should also be prevented.

2.   Central or chapter heading should not be underlined.

Use of Apostrophe

Correct use of apostrophe is preferred. It is used in possessive forms and also in contracted forms, and not in words

ending in s.

For example:

    a.   I drove my brother's car.

    b.   James' house

    c.   Employees' morale

    d.   '98 (= 1998)

Use of Passive Voice

Use of passive voice is preferred in writing the report. If you want to indicate or imply that something is an opinion which is held by an unspecified group of people, you can use a passive form of reporting verb with it as the impersonal subject.

For example:

    a.   It was found that.....

    b.   Respondents' were of the view that......

    c.   It was reported by the respondents that......

Revision is.....

Revision is an important feature of good report writing – even experienced researchers with many publications revise their reports many times before giving them for final typing.

Final word.....

It is always advisable to show the report to learned friends or language experts for correction before it is finallytyped.

5.4 Use of Computers in research: data collection and analysis

In research, computers play an important role. Even though computer technology has changed dramatically over time, the rationale for the use of computers has remained the same. Computers are tools that help us to store, process, access and analysis data more quickly and easily. Using statistical methods today generally means applying a statistical computer program. Many excellent statistical packages are available both for mainframe and personal computers. Among the widely used packages are SPSS, SAS, MINITAB and many others.

Data collection and Analysis

An example of data entry package is SPSS (Statistical Package for the Social Sciences) Data Entry, which includes user-friendly facilities for data input and editing. Computer packages handling the actual statistical analysis come in two basic forms: specialized programs, focusing on a particular application and general programs, offering a wide variety of facilities. Research finding must be reported. Pages and pages of computer printout are not easily readable.